IMAGES
of America

JOHNSTON
COUNTY

Selma Elementary School
(Grandaddy attended)

This book is dedicated to Harold M. Medlin, photographer, local historian, and former member of the Johnston County Board of Education, whose generosity and technical knowledge of photographic reproduction have helped to make this book possible. (Courtesy of Four Oaks-Benson *News-in-Review*.)

Cover photograph: In 1908 Mina Johnson, pictured in back to the right, began her fifty-year teaching career with these students at Four Oaks School. In those days boys sat on one side of the room, while girls sat on the other.

IMAGES
of America

JOHNSTON COUNTY

Todd Johnson and Durwood Barbour

ARCADIA

ISBN 0-7524-0817-8

Published by Arcadia Publishing,
an imprint of the Chalford Publishing Corporation,
One Washington Center, Dover, New Hampshire 03820.
Printed in Great Britain

Library of Congress Cataloging-in-Publication Data applied for

The North Carolina Railroad (NCRR) was the first of many major developments in transportation that have brought the greatest changes to Johnston County's landscape. The NCRR locomotive shown here was named in honor of Boon Hill Township's William A. Smith (1828–1888), noted Republican politician during the Civil War and Reconstruction era. He served as Confederate militia commander (1861–1865), president of the North Carolina Railroad (1868–1873), and member of the 43rd U.S. Congress (1873–1875). (Courtesy of William W. Smith.)

4

Contents

Acknowledgments

This pictorial history of a period in Johnston County's life was conceived as an effort by our citizens to record in graphic form the life of our people through 1945. Indeed it has been a collective effort by its citizens. Many pictures were loaned or donated by individuals and institutions. These contributors are named at the end of each caption.

It has been a special pleasure to collaborate on this project with Todd Johnson, curator of the Johnston County Room. He is a young man with a long, abiding love for Johnston County and its people.

Some of the people who made constructive suggestions or gave us information on their community or particular photographs are Vernon Creech, Alton Fitzgerald, Harry Hill, Claudia Brown, Norman Anderson, Harold Medlin, Reid Barbour, Virginia Satterfield, Betty Coats, Maurice Toler, Ray Hodge, Merlin and Peggy Thompson, and Roland Jackson. Saundra Freeman's help with photograph finishing when we were "in a pinch" was crucial.

Much of the information in these pages has come from a core group of dedicated local historians, past and present, to whom we owe a debt of gratitude. They are Thomas Lassiter, Wingate Lassiter, Calvin Edgerton, Col. Robert Boyette, James Bryan Creech, Dr. James Batten, Carolyn Ennis, William Norris, John A. Mitchiner, Herschel Rose, C. Stanton Coats, John T. Talton, Virginia Satterfield, Claudia S. Brown, and Edith S. Johnson.

A special thanks must go to our friend Stephen Massengill of the North Carolina Division of Archives and History for his help in searching their inventory for Johnston County photos and producing copies for us.

Margaret McLemore Lee of the Johnston County Room was invaluable with her vast storehouse of Johnston County history—much of which she has in her "human" computer. I never cease to be amazed by her enthusiastic and graceful responses to citizens from near and far in their quest for information about their family or local history.

To my wife, Mary Anne Barbour, I extend my deepest gratitude for her support, suggestions, and many hours entering my written work into the computer. Then there were more hours spent proofreading and making corrections.

Lastly, I am humbled by the efforts made by our ancestral families, friends, and people we have only read about, who lived through economic depression, wars, as well as good times in order that we might live the good life. Research (reading and talking with people) for this book has given me a greater appreciation for their role in enabling us to have a better today and tomorrow—that is really what this book is about. Many thanks to them.

M. Durwood Barbour

Introduction

The story of Johnston County is that of a diverse people with strong ties to their land, families, and communities. These ties have kept agriculture the primary economic pursuit and the landscape predominantly rural for over two and a half centuries. While large-scale agricultural operations have supplanted the family farms which were once the county's mainstay, there are still a surprising number of farms that several generations have owned for a century or more.

Johnston County's first farmers were primarily subsistence producers, growing little more than was required to feed and clothe their families. Some made profits by raising large herds of swine and cattle, which they drove to markets in Virginia. A few grew tobacco, which they hauled on wagons to Virginia or shipped down the Neuse River to New Bern, and from there to Norfolk.

Smithfield, the county seat, became important to inland trade in North Carolina because it was the westernmost navigable point on the Neuse for freight-carrying vessels. In 1770 the colonial assembly attempted to boost North Carolina's tobacco trade by erecting a warehouse near Smithfield for receiving and storing tobacco before it was shipped to Virginia. Nonetheless, it would be another century and a quarter before this product would gain the attention of Johnston's commercial farmers.

Following the introduction of Eli Whitney's gin in Johnston County around 1804, cotton gradually became the county's leading money crop. Corn was also produced for market, although profits were small in comparison to the white, fleecy staple. Before the 1850s, poor roads leading to distant markets were a deterrent to commercial farming. The completion of the 223-mile North Carolina Railroad in 1856 placed Johnston County inside the prosperous Piedmont Crescent, between Goldsboro and Charlotte, and this meant an eventual shift from subsistence farming to market-driven agriculture. In addition to boosting cotton and grain productions, this railroad spurred growth in the turpentine and lumber industries. The railroad also gave rise to towns at Princeton, Pine Level, Selma, and Clayton in the 1860s and 1870s.

During the Civil War, Johnstonians saw some 1,500 of their sons, husbands, fathers, and brothers go off to fight. Almost a third of these men died in service, and many of those returning suffered from physical disabilities. Emancipation of slaves and political turmoil further exacerbated the social and economic tensions that would not diminish significantly until the turn of the twentieth century. In 1868 a new state constitution would bring into being Johnston's first townships: "Bentonsville," Beulah, Boon Hill, Clayton, Elevation, Ingrams, Meadow, O'Neals, Pleasant Grove, Selma, Smithfield, and Wilders. Between 1887 and 1913, parts of these would be taken to form Wilson's Mills, Cleveland, Banner, Pine Level, and Micro.

In 1886 the Wilmington and Weldon Railroad completed a second major line through Johnston County, which the Atlantic Coastline Railroad soon acquired. Called the Short-Cut, it provided quicker travel from the north into South Carolina than the previous route, which had passed through Goldsboro and Wilmington. The towns of Kenly, Micro, Four Oaks, and Benson grew up along this line.

With two major railroads intersecting at Selma, Johnston was poised for unprecedented commercial and industrial growth, and within a decade that growth began to take place. A depression in 1893 and a resulting plummet in cotton prices forced many local farmers to look for another money crop. The success of bright leaf tobacco growers in the piedmont areas of North Carolina and Virginia soon began to catch on in Johnston and other eastern North Carolina counties in the 1890s, to the extent that a market for the leaf was established in Smithfield in 1898. The county's first bank, by no coincidence, was also established that year. Within a few years cotton mills had been built and put in operation in Smithfield, Clayton, and Selma, and telephone lines were extended to practically every town. Within a couple of decades Johnston townsfolk would have electric lights and running water. It was a time of great optimism, at least for those who had wealth and those who aspired to it. The array of stately homes in both town and country, brick stores, paved streets, schools, and churches of the 1920s had certainly reached a level higher than those of only a generation earlier.

World War I sent some 1,000 young Johnstonians into military service, about fifty of whom paid the supreme sacrifice. Though it displaced manpower, the war also further boosted the local economy by bringing a surge, albeit short-lived, in cotton and tobacco prices. The resulting prosperity fostered a progressive spirit across the county and state that brought revolutionary changes in education and transportation.

In 1920 Johnston had ninety-nine schools for white students and thirty-five for black students, most of which were housed in ill-equipped wooden buildings with one or two teachers. A local committee controlled each school, and special taxes approved at the district level dictated the size and quality of each school. When County School Superintendent H.B. Marrow took office in 1922, he set out to bridge the gaps between whites and blacks and between town and country in the public educational system. In only a decade he was able to oversee not only the largest school-building campaign in the county's history, but also the abandonment of autonomous districts in favor of a county school system that could more equally distribute educational resources.

When the postwar boom put extra money in many local pockets, those funds were spent mostly on automobiles. Ford Models A and T were the most affordable, hence the most popular. Merchants and other businessmen throughout the state soon realized that in order to get people to drive into town more often they needed better roads, so their friends in the state legislature of 1921 authorized a $50-million bond issue for statewide road construction. As a result, two paved state highways came through Johnston. An east-west NC 10 (later rerouted to become U.S. 70.) came through Princeton, Pine Level, Selma, Smithfield, and Clayton, and a north-south NC 22 (rerouted in 1935 to become U.S. 301) passed through Kenly, Micro, Selma, Smithfield, Four Oaks, and Benson. Towns soon began paving streets, and businesses boomed as never before.

Despite good fortune in commercial centers, farmers in the 1920s were suffering under a postwar agricultural depression that brought dramatic fluctuations in cotton and tobacco prices. According to the U.S. Census Bureau, the number of mortgaged farms in the county grew from 793 in 1925 to 1,124 in 1930. The percentage of farms operated by tenants also jumped from an already high fifty-one in 1920 to fifty-nine in 1930. Cotton farmers tried to make up for their losses by overproducing, a practice that only served to drive market prices even lower.

The stock market crash of 1929 and Great Depression that followed intensified the hard times farmers were already experiencing. Most banks closed, and wealthy families in practically every town saw their fortunes literally disappear. The boll weevil joined forces with federal crop controls in dethroning King Cotton in Johnston County. While many farmers then turned to tobacco, market prices for the golden leaf remained low through the 1930s. Nevertheless, a combination of federal programs and firmly entrenched interdependence among families and neighborhoods saw people through this difficult era and prepared them for yet another trying time.

World War II sent an astonishing 7,000 Johnston County men and women into military service, at least 140 of whom died in service. The war also displaced many others who left for war-related jobs in cities. Those left at home faced the challenges of keeping farms, businesses, schools, churches, and other institutions and organizations running, all the while coping with rationing and other exigencies of war.

Smithfield's annual Farmer's Day celebration on August 15, 1945, turned out to be "the most celebrated day in Johnston County history," as county historians Tom and Wingate Lassiter point out. During the previous evening, President Truman had announced the Japanese surrender and the end of war. Those who lived through the Great Depression and the World War would no doubt agree with the Lassiters' statement that it was truly "the most defining moment" in the county's history.

The book concludes at this juncture. Perhaps a sequel will be possible in the near future to bring to life events that would continue to shape this land called Johnston County.

K. Todd Johnson
August 1997

This is an Elevation Township tobacco field in the 1930s. (Courtesy of Harold Medlin.)

Ava Lavinia Gardner (1922–1990), who grew up in Johnston's rural Brogden community, is Johnston's most famous native of all time. She was propelled to Hollywood stardom in 1941 soon after an errand clerk for Metro Goldwyn Mayer saw this photo in the window of her brother-in-law's New York photography studio in 1941. (Courtesy of Ava Gardner Museum.)

In September 1884, North Carolinians held a four-week Great State Exposition in Raleigh so counties could show each other and the rest of the country what they had to offer. As evidenced in this photo and in an October 22, 1915 *Smithfield Herald* article by John A. Mitchener, Johnston County prided itself in items such as cotton bales, wood products, embroidery, vinegar, cider, wine, whiskey, and brandy. Mitchener displayed a bottle of the 1884 vinegar at the County Fair in 1915. For a long time he had kept bottles of the various wines, whiskeys, and brandies, but "somehow or another these bottles leaked," and they were not available for show in 1915. (Courtesy of N.C. Division of Archives and History.)

One
Rural Communities

Before the state began maintaining roads in the late 1910s, local men were required to repair them. About 1905 these men were shown taking their turn on the Averasboro Road near Elevation Methodist Church. (Courtesy of Harold Medlin.)

This covered bridge over the Neuse River was the main link to Clayton for folks in Archer Lodge and other northwestern Johnston communities in the nineteenth and early twentieth centuries. Heavy rains would sometimes make it virtually impossible to cross. (Courtesy of Johnston County Room.)

Built around 1883, the same Neuse River Bridge shown above is pictured not long before being torn down in 1938. It was the last covered bridge in Johnston County. (Courtesy of Johnston County Room.)

Motoring along soft soil roads such as this one in an unknown part of Johnston was difficult in dry weather and sometimes impossible after heavy rains. By the mid-1920s, east-west North Carolina 10 (currently U.S. 70), north-south North Carolina 22 (currently U.S. 301), and many of the towns' main streets had been paved. However, most of the county roads and many town streets remained poorly maintained and unpaved until the legislature passed a 1949 bond issue. (Courtesy of North Carolina Division of Archives and History.)

The Wilson's Mills depot on the North Carolina/Southern Railroad is shown here about 1910. The wagon-load of lumber no doubt came from the Wilsons' nearby sawmill. Dr. Carlton Adams (1906–1994) recalled "white" and "colored" waiting rooms, with large wood stoves for heat and kerosene wall lamps for light. In the same building, freight was received and stored until picked up. In the 1920s passenger fare from Clayton to Wilson's Mills was 25¢. (Courtesy of Charles Wilson.)

This baptism occurred at an unknown Johnston County location in the early 1900s. Since Primitive Baptists, Missionary Baptists, and Free Will Baptists were Johnston's predominant religious groups in the nineteenth and early twentieth centuries, scenes of the newly converted being baptized by immersion in rivers, creeks, or mill ponds were common in the warm months. (Courtesy of Johnston County Room.)

Wesley Mitchiner (c. 1864–1936) was a unique character in the rural African-American community of Graytown near Smithfield. He was best remembered for his extensive knowledge of the Bible, and he also studied dictionaries so much that he had an unusually large vocabulary. He made a living at gardening, cutting wood, and performing other odd jobs he could find around the county seat. (Courtesy of Johnston County Room.)

Some members of Wilders Township's White Oak Baptist Church, established in 1859, posed in front of their newly-completed sanctuary about 1912. By that time Gothic windows and doors were in vogue. Church records from 1910 indicate the building was valued at $1,500 and had a seating capacity of five hundred. The church membership stood at 186 that year, with 79 males and 107 females. (Courtesy of Charles H. Johnson.)

Pisgah Baptist Church in Smithfield Township, shown here about 1930, was one of Johnston County's most progressive rural congregations in the early twentieth century. In about 1916, Pisgah, along with Shiloh, Baptist Center, and Wilson's Mills churches, built what was touted as one of the first rural parsonages in the state. Under the leadership of Rev. S.S. McGregor, (1925–1930), the church increased services from one to two Sundays a month, built seven classrooms, and purchased the three Sunday school trucks shown here. (Courtesy of Johnston County Room.)

Garner A. Smith's general store, shown here about 1909, was located about one mile west of Bethesda Baptist Church on the Raleigh-to-Smithfield Road (present Hwy 70 Business). Such establishments, where one could find everything from A to Z, were common on the rural landscape between the Civil War and the Great Depression. The advent of automobiles and paved highways would mark a decline in the number of country merchants such as Mr. Smith. (Courtesy of Grace Smith.)

The legendary J. Percy Flowers (1903–1982), tobacco farmer, store owner, pillar of White Oak Baptist Church, and head of a nationally-known bootleg empire, is pictured here in the early 1930s in front of his general store in Wilders Township. In a March 28, 1993 *News and Observer* article, Mrs. Flowers recalled that "he knew what it was like to be a boy with no money and to go into a store and just stare at the candy with no way to get any. Any child that walked into his store got a couple of pieces of candy." (Courtesy of Johnston County Room.)

16

Polenta Academy and Lodge in Cleveland Township was built in 1891 and burned in the 1950s. Local Masons used the second floor until the 1920s. The college preparatory school on the first floor was in operation until the first decade of the twentieth century. (Courtesy of Genevieve Honeycutt.)

This hog-killing on the John Hardy Barefoot farm in Meadow Township took place around the turn of the twentieth century. In the foreground is a barrel, tilted and partially buried, where hogs were immersed in scalding water to remove their hair after being killed. Like the corn-shucking, it was a neighborhood event that involved both work and socializing, as evidenced in this rare photograph. (Courtesy of Johnston County Room.)

Dr. George A. McLemore came to Johnston fresh out of medical school in 1906 and soon took over Dr. E.N. Booker's practice in Cleveland, Pleasant Grove, and Elevation Townships. He is shown here with his wife, Nellie, and daughter, Margaret, in 1911 at their home in Cleveland. At left is the office where he received patients, although he primarily made house calls. In 1916 he had a private telephone line run to his home from Benson so his more distant patients would not have to lose time traveling to get him in emergencies. (Courtesy of Johnston County Room.)

Before Governor Charles B. Aycock launched an aggressive school-building campaign in 1900, many rural families hired their own teachers or sent their children to private schools. Confederate veteran Ransom Penny of near Clayton built this simple one-room school on his farm, probably in the 1880s. His children are pictured with their teacher around 1890. (Courtesy of Jackie Cannon.)

This public school for whites in O'Neals Township District 1 was built in 1908 at a cost of $450. Local citizens provided this school for their children by voting in a property tax of 25¢ per $100 valuation. It was called Thanksgiving School because it was located near Thanksgiving Baptist Church. With two rooms and a vestibule, it completed its first year of operation with two teachers, an enrollment of eighty-one, and average attendance of forty-five. (Courtesy of Johnston County Room.)

Polenta School for whites, originally located near Oakland Presbyterian Church in Cleveland Township, is thought to have been built sometime in the 1880s. A photographer caught these children playing in the schoolyard in the first decade of the twentieth century. (Courtesy of Charles Tomlinson.)

This photograph from the 1910s or 1920s is thought to be of students at Galilee School in Smithfield Township. The photograph was in the possession of Grace Smith Rembert, whose mother, Louisa Sanders Smith, taught at Galilee. A 1908–1909 county school report shows Mrs. Smith teaching at Smithfield Township District 4 with an enrollment of forty-five and average attendance of twenty. Students from the school were sent to Short Journey when it opened in 1927. (Courtesy of Thelma Wall.)

Students at Skinner's "College" in Beulah Township are shown performing morning calisthenics in 1922. Dr. J.H. Skinner began his career as a taxi driver in New York City before coming to the Kenly area. Since there was no public high school for African-Americans here, the Free Will Baptist Conference (black) established this school for both elementary and secondary grades about 1914, with Dr. Skinner in charge. It closed about 1930. Many students came from surrounding counties and boarded with local families. (Courtesy of Grethel Boyette.)

Students at Pleasant Grove School for white students posed for this photograph in about 1912. A few of the students were older than the teacher. (Courtesy of Annie Stephenson King and Claudia Stephenson Brown.)

Students at Polenta Graded School for whites in Cleveland Township are pictured here in 1916. By that time, the school had been relocated from Oakland Church to the J. Walter Myatt farm on what is now Polenta Road. (Courtesy of Margaret McLemore Lee.)

In 1922 these students met at Pleasant Grove School in Pleasant Grove Township to take the county's seventh-grade examination. They came from schools at Piney Grove, Ogburn Grove, Piney Forest, Rehobeth, High Tower, Wildwood, Sunny Nook, and Mount Zion as well as Pleasant Grove. (Courtesy of Edith Stephenson Johnson.)

Teachers and students at Royall School for whites in Boon Hill Township were captured in this photograph in the mid-1920s. (Courtesy of Johnston County Room.)

Corinth-Holder's School for whites, located at the border of Wilders and O'Neals Townships, was built in 1923. Instead of selecting a more central location, the school board chose a site near Corinth. In retaliation, an unknown person or persons dynamited a corner of the building as it neared completion. The school was completed, despite threatening notes sent to workers, and opened in 1924. (Courtesy of Johnston County Room.)

Brogden School for white students in Boon Hill Township was completed and opened for the 1924 school year. The teacher's residence at left was the childhood home of film star Ava Gardner, whose mother operated the boardinghouse for teachers. Ava was said to have climbed to the top of the water tower (background center) as a little girl. The school burned in the 1980s. (Courtesy of Johnston County Room.)

The 1927 fourth-grade class of Brogden School posed for this photograph with teacher Thelma Keene (back row center) and mascot Ava Gardner (front row, fifth from right), who was about four years old at the time. The photograph was donated to the Ava Gardner Museum in Smithfield in 1996 and put on display only minutes before an elderly visitor arrived, identifying herself as a former teacher at Brogden. The museum hostess was astonished when she learned the visitor was Thelma Keene. (Courtesy of Ava Gardner Museum.)

When the state appropriated funds for the first public high schools in 1907, Wilson's Mills was one of three (all white) that the Johnston County Board of Education chose to receive; the others were Benson and Kenly. This structure, completed in 1904, was built at a cost of nearly $2,500, paid for by a property tax of 30¢ per $100 valuation that Wilson's Mills residents approved in a 1901 referendum. This three-teacher school, in use until the 1920s, had three rooms on the first floor, a large hall, cloak room, and auditorium. (Courtesy of Johnston County Room.)

This brick consolidated school for whites at Wilson's Mills, completed in 1924, replaced the frame structure in use during the previous twenty years. The old building was sold for $2,000. This three-story brick building served elementary and high school students until Smithfield-Selma High School opened in 1969. It continued in use as an elementary school for another twenty-five years and was demolished to make way for a modern one-story elementary school. (Courtesy of Johnston County Room.)

The 1931 graduating class of Wilson's Mills High School posed with their teacher and principal in front of the teacher's residence. Graduate Edna Alford Wilder (front row, left) says the class of twelve would have numbered only six if Four Oaks School had not transferred her and five others to Wilson's Mills a year earlier to alleviate overcrowding. (Courtesy of Edna Alford Caudill Wilder.)

Archer Lodge School for whites in Wilders Township was constructed in 1923 and demolished in 1974. In the left background is the boardinghouse for teachers. (Courtesy of Johnston County Room.)

Meadow School for white students was constructed at Peacock's Crossroads in Meadow Township in 1924. This three-story building, originally equipped with twenty-one classrooms, an office, library, laboratories, and 1,100-seat auditorium, is among the dwindling number of 1920s schools still in use. Graduate Budd Smith stated in a 1956 graduation speech that A.G. Glenn, the first principal, "inspired and motivated more young people to go forward in the academic world than probably any principal in North Carolina." (Courtesy of Johnston County Room.)

Dorothy Hooks captured these students at Short Journey School for blacks in Smithfield Township around 1945. The school was completed in 1927 with the help of the Julius Rosenwald Fund and was in operation until racial segregation ended in Johnston in 1969. Eva Johnson Cooper (1903–1995) served as principal during the school's entire history. The building is now owned by the Raleigh Catholic Diocese and serves as a Christian retreat center. (Courtesy of Johnston County Room.)

This Dorothy Hooks photograph of students at Short Journey School is also dated around 1945. (Courtesy of Johnston County Room.)

Gristmills were common on the rural landscape prior to World War II. Barber Mill, pictured here about 1920, was built shortly after B.T. Barber got a license from the County in 1879 to dam up a section of Swift Creek, where it separates Cleveland and Clayton Townships. He not only ground corn here but also operated a sawmill. The mill pond was widely known as a good place for shad fishing. (Courtesy of Edward Barber.)

Leon Parker and his wife, Annie, enjoyed the serenity of a boat ride on Parker Mill Pond in Meadow Township, sometime around their marriage in 1921. The Parkers have owned the mill since 1867. In addition to recreational uses such as fishing and swimming, it has also been used by local churches for baptisms. (Courtesy of Estelle Parker Blackman.)

Two
The County Seat

SMITHFIELD, N. C.
ohnston County Court House

This brick courthouse, which stood at the southeast corner of Market and Second Streets, was the county's epicenter from 1843 to 1921. The fates of orphans, slaves, paupers, criminals, and others at the mercy of the legal system were decided here. The most far-reaching event took place there in 1865, when General William T. Sherman stood here in front of his army and announced the news of General Robert E. Lee's surrender. (Courtesy of Johnston County Room.)

Members of the courthouse ring were captured as they relaxed in front of the old brick courthouse in May 1902. Ornate exterior stairways (one partially visible to the right) leading to the second floor were added in the 1880s, when county leaders voted to dismantle the original interior stairs to allow additional floor space. (Courtesy of Johnston County Room.)

Rural students at Smithfield Training School for blacks (renamed Johnston County Training School in 1922) roomed in this dormitory between the 1910s and 1930s. It was located on the site of the present Opportunity Building in the Belmont section of Smithfield. This school, which began in 1914, was the first high school in Johnston County for African Americans. Since state funds were not made available for blacks when the first public high schools were funded, its earliest financing came from private sources such as the Johnston District Baptist Association. (Courtesy of Johnston County Room.)

The Pomona-Creech Home Demonstration Club and string band, pictured here on the courthouse steps, performed a two-act play, *Line and Color*, on Home Demonstration Achievement Day in June 1926. Since the day's activities centered around clothing, the play was performed to demonstrate the importance of line and color in dress. County-wide events such as this one were usually held at the courthouse or some other central location in the county seat. (Courtesy of Johnston County Room.)

Johnston County Hospital, depicted here on a *c.* 1930 postcard, was dedicated April 19, 1926. Funds were raised for its construction by sale of stock. The first chief surgeon was Dr. W.J.B. Orr, who served until 1929, when he sold his stock to Dr. Vartan A. Davidian and moved to Washington, D.C. Dr. Davidian, born of Armenian parents in Rhode Island, served as chief surgeon until his retirement in 1974. The Department of Social Services is now located in the building shown here. (Courtesy of Mamie Edwards Johnson.)

From 1941 to 1967, separate Smithfield and Johnston County libraries existed side by side on Johnston Street behind the courthouse. At the urging of School Superintendent Adolph Vermont, a group of young ladies began the town's collection in 1912, and after various locations, it was moved to Johnston Street in 1939. The County established its library and bookmobile service in 1941, shortly after the General Assembly approved state aid for public libraries. Smithfield's Lawrence H. Wallace was the legislator who introduced the library aid bill. (Courtesy of Johnston County Room.)

Some seven hundred seventh graders from throughout the county, pictured here, converged at Turlington Graded School on South Third Street to take the high school entrance examination in about 1925. A special "Opportunities in Johnston County" edition of the *Smithfield Herald* in 1928 states that 513 students passed. Before the exam was made a requirement in 1923, few students pursued secondary education. For instance, in 1920, only forty-two seventh graders were promoted to high school. (Courtesy of Johnston County Room.)

The prime movers of the school consolidation movement of the 1920s are pictured here in front of Smithfield High School on South Second Street. The school was built in 1922, the same year Henry B. Marrow (second from right) was appointed county school superintendent. Between 1922 and 1930, he and his staff took 134 small schools and consolidated them into 23 large ones. School trucks such as the ones shown here were vital to this revolution in the educational system. (Courtesy of Johnston County Room.)

Smithfield (now First) Baptist Church, organized in 1832, worshipped in this building on the northwest corner of Church and Second Streets from 1835 to 1903. During a period of decline in the 1870s, no services were held, but an elderly lady named Patsy Crocker swept the floors every Saturday, praying that the church would be revived. When another denomination tried to organize in the building, she went and claimed it for the Baptists. Today it is Johnston's largest church. (Courtesy of Johnston County Room.)

This dinner on the grounds is thought to be a Smithfield Baptist Sunday school picnic from around 1900. Identifiable church leaders are Jim Beaty (in foreground) and F.H. Brooks (lying on ground). (Courtesy of Luby Royall Jr.)

Smithfield (now Centenary) Methodist Church worshipped in this well-shaded sanctuary on North Second Street from 1895 to 1914, when they moved to their current location at the corner of Market and Second. Located on the same site that the Methodists had used since organizing in the county seat in 1839, this building replaced a tall one-room structure which had a slave gallery. The house to the left, still standing, was the L.R. Waddell home, an expanded antebellum office building dating to around 1850. (Courtesy of Marsha Hood Brewer.)

St. Mark's African Methodist Episcopal Church built this sanctuary about 1910 at the Bridge (originally Smith) Street location, where the congregation still worships. It was enlarged and remodeled in the popular Gothic style in 1924, with Rev. Gore, the pastor, supervising and performing much of the work. Dr. John B. Beckwith conveyed the 1/4-acre lot to the AME Conference in 1882. (Courtesy of Helen Holt.)

From 1905 to 1926, this stately opera house adorned the west side of South Third Street's 100 block, serving as town hall, meat market, and auditorium. The first floor housed the town clerk, police, jail, and meat cutter. The second floor was the auditorium, with third floor balcony. Atop the building was a tower containing the fire bell. A generation of Smithfield residents enjoyed traveling shows, silent movies, local talent, musicals, and public gatherings here until fire destroyed the building following an Armistice Day event. (Courtesy of Johnston County Room.)

J. Bryant Alford, a free black during slavery and Johnston's first African-American merchant, built this covered bridge over the Neuse shortly after the Civil War. At that time the river crossing was at Smith (now Bridge) Street. This single-lane bridge was replaced by a steel, two-lane bridge in 1907. (Courtesy of Johnston County Room.)

This steel bridge over the Neuse at Bridge Street was built in 1907 by Austin Brothers of Atlanta, Georgia. Construction cost county taxpayers some $8,000 and took about four months to complete. It was dismantled only some fifteen years later when State Highway No. 10 was paved and routed down Market Street. (Courtesy of Durwood Barbour.)

Smithfield Collegiate Institute was established in 1886 by Ira Turlington and John Davis. In 1891, the building shown here on a 1905-vintage postcard was erected on South Third Street and the name was changed to Turlington Institute. The school changed from private status in 1903 and became Turlington Graded School, offering free elementary and secondary education to white students. (Courtesy of Durwood Barbour.)

This bird's-eye view of Smithfield was taken from the tower of Turlington Institute about 1910. To the right is South Third Street, as it heads north into downtown. In the left background, Riverside Cemetery and St. Paul's Episcopal Church are visible. (Courtesy of Gordon Hudson.)

Turlington Institute offered a military department for male students, complete with Springfield breech-loading rifles and standard military equipment. Cadets such as the ones pictured here *c.* 1901 boarded in barracks behind the school and performed daily drill exercises. An 1892 school catalogue states that in addition to "training them to walk erect and carry themselves more gracefully," the exercises helped "to control them." (Courtesy of W. Don Mason.)

The Tuscarora Inn, shown here on a 1912 postcard, was the pride of Smithfield when it opened at the northeast corner of Market and Second Streets in January 1902. Four stories high, it had twenty-six elegantly furnished rooms, waterworks, and electric call bells. The first floor housed stores and offices, and salesmen, tobacco buyers, and other business people lodged on the upper floors. The Smithfield Improvement Company underwrote the $14,000 facility mainly to boost the town's tobacco market. (Courtesy of Durwood Barbour.)

This pre-automobile Smithfield street scene shows South Third Street shortly after the first telephone lines were installed in 1898. At left is E.J. Holt's hardware store and livery stables. Mr. Holt also sold Babcock carriages. Next is a grocery store (according to 1901 Sanborn insurance map), which advertised stoves. Beyond the alley is the original home of the Bank of Smithfield (later First Citizens Bank). The man in the foreground with lamp in hand is painter C.W. Lindsey. (Courtesy of Johnston County Room.)

Facing west in this postcard view are Hood's Drug Store, the domes of the old brick courthouse and Methodist church on the left, and the First National Bank and Creech's Drug Store on the right. The card is postmarked, "Wilson's Mills, North Carolina, September 27, 1915." This date was shortly after the town's first electric lines and streetlights were installed. Postcards of this unknown photographer's work also have been found depicting North Carolina scenes in Garner, Apex, and Belmont. (Courtesy of Durwood Barbour.)

Townsmen in front of Dr. Thel Hooks's office at the southwest corner of Third and Market Streets enjoyed the snow in this *c.* 1910 scene. The Hooks office was in the former home of T.R. Hood's Drug Store, which had recently moved to an adjacent building. Across the street is the J.H. Edgerton livery stable, with vacant lot in front where the Bank of Smithfield and the Cotter-Underwood building would be constructed in 1914. (Courtesy of Johnston County Room.)

Smithfield's Lyric Theatre, left, one of Johnston's first movie houses, opened in 1916 at this location on the northwest corner of Third and Johnston Streets. The Lyric's earliest movies included Sammie Burns in *The Dawgone Dog* (1916), Douglas Fairbanks in *Double Trouble* (1919), and Theda Bara in *Cleopatra* (1919). Hunter Ellington operated a livery, insurance, and real estate business next door. (Courtesy of Johnston County Room.)

Three
North Carolina Railroad Towns:
Princeton, Selma, Clayton, Pine Level

This photograph postcard from 1915 shows Princeton, Johnston's second oldest town, in the days before paved streets. Ed A. Holt (right), standing next to his store entrance, owned and operated this general merchandise business until his death in 1932. The building is still in use. (Courtesy of North Carolina Museum of History.)

The brick portion of the building seen here was erected in Princeton in 1916 by John Ledbetter, who operated a general store. In 1936, Carl and Gardner Gurley purchased the store and soon built a corn meal and feed mill as an adjunct to the general merchandise business. In 1944 they sold their store merchandise and began purchasing plants in Washington, Goldsboro, and Selma, North Carolina; Florence, South Carolina; and Talladega, Alabama. (Courtesy of Merlin and Peggy Gurley Thompson.)

Selma's Union Station, shown here on a *c.* 1910 postcard, was built by the Southern and Atlantic Coastline railroad companies in 1896, immediately after Southern Railway leased the North Carolina Railroad. During the previous decade, the two railroads had maintained separate passenger depots, forcing travelers to hire a hack or walk when changing stations. This building was replaced with the present station in 1924. (Courtesy of Lynette and Allen Wilson.)

Selma's stately Town Hall and Opera House with clock tower was constructed in 1916 and is shown here in the late 1930s. The auditorium, on the second floor, was used for meetings, plays, movies, and other entertainment for many years before the building fell into disrepair. This important landmark was torn down in 1971. (Courtesy of North Carolina Division of Archives and History.)

This postcard, postmarked 1909, shows the short-lived drugstore Edward W. Vick operated on Raiford Street in Selma before relocating to Goldsboro. Vick's VapoRub, which Edward's uncle Lunsford Richardson made a household word, was named in honor of his father, Dr. Joshua Vick. Childhood pictures of Edward; his brother, George; and sister, Eudora, were used as part of the Vick's trademark during the early years of Vick Chemical Company. (Courtesy of Vernon Creech.)

The Selma Tomato, Melon, and Better Baby Fair was a beehive of activity on July 24, 1915. Held annually from 1912 to 1917, the highlight was a contest between thirty to fifty babies from across Johnston County. (Courtesy of North Carolina Division of Archives and History.)

Roberts, Corbett and Woodard in Selma sold groceries, clothing, and farm machinery, as shown here about the time of World War I. Also depicted are two Model T Ford touring cars of *c.* 1918 vintage and an adjacent insurance company offering to buy Liberty Bonds. (Courtesy of Mildred P. Lee.)

The hotel shown here on a 1909 vintage postcard was built in 1903 on Selma's East Railroad Street. The location was near Union Station at the intersection of both railroads. (Courtesy of Durwood Barbour.)

Selma (now Edgerton Memorial) Methodist Church, built in 1910 at the corner of Sumner and Anderson Streets, is shown in this postcard with a 1912 postmark. An earlier sanctuary dating from 1878, which originally faced Sumner Street, is also shown facing Anderson Street behind the new building. (Courtesy of Vernon Creech.)

The 1924 freshman class of Selma's High School for black students posed with teacher Idella McCreary (back row, fourth from left) and principal J.R. Dupree (back row, fifth from left.) The building, in use from about 1915 to 1933, was the former Selma Academy, which moved to this site on West Watson Street. It burned in 1933, and the Richard B. Harrison School was built on the site in 1935. (Courtesy of Irving G. Bell.)

Selma High School's Class of 1919 was all girls, no doubt due to the boys' involvement in World War I service. This was also before the high school entrance examination was required of all Johnston County seventh graders. (Courtesy of Myrtle Ricks Rose.)

The people shown here in this 1914 photograph gathered to worship in an open shelter. The man to the far right was George Brietz, superintendent of the Selma Cotton Mill. He is credited with the formation of the congregation, and when a permanent structure was built at 910 Railroad Street, the church was named Brietz Chapel. It was later destroyed. Currently, the Church of Faith is located on that site. (Courtesy of Johnston County Room.)

Gurkin's Tavern, cabins, and service station were located on the west side of U.S. 301, near its intersection with U.S. 70 just south of Selma. This complex, shown here in about 1940, was known as Catch-Me-Eye. The service station was completely destroyed when a munitions truck exploded about 100 yards to the north in 1942. (Courtesy of Durwood Barbour.)

Hotel Talton was located on the east side of U.S. 301 at the site of the 1942 munitions truck explosion. Four people were killed in the hotel, which was totally destroyed. (Courtesy of Durwood Barbour.)

When daylight appeared on March 7, 1942, Catch-Me-Eye looked like a war zone. After colliding with a car and catching on fire, the truck, loaded with 30,000 pounds of munitions, exploded at 2:47 am. (Courtesy of Rose Sugg Bryan.)

The Catch-Me-Eye explosion left a basin in U.S. 301 large enough to bury a railroad freight car. Thousands came to see the devastation. Seven people were killed, more than a hundred were injured, and many structures were damaged in the Selma area. (Courtesy of Rose Sugg Bryan.)

World War II was raging, and almost everything citizens saw, heard, or talked about was war. When that huge explosion at Catch-Me-Eye rattled windows for many miles and was heard as far away as Raleigh and Fayetteville, many were fearful that an air raid had occurred. They had a psychological need to see that, while the event was tragic, the war had not actually reached our shores. (Courtesy of Rose Sugg Bryan.)

This postcard showing Clayton's Depot Square is undated but was published *c*. 1910. The depot made a thriving watermelon business possible. In 1908 farmers shipped 105 carloads of watermelons from here. The large building to the right was the Robertson Hotel, which was owned by Dr. James Battle Robertson. (Courtesy of Durwood Barbour.)

The Ashley Horne mansion in Clayton, built during the years 1894 to 1897, is shown here around 1910. It was said to have been constructed of eleven types of wood cut within a 2-mile radius. Mr. Horne was a farmer, merchant, banker, and industrial leader. He became a state senator, and in 1908 made an unsuccessful bid for governor of North Carolina. (Courtesy of Durwood Barbour.)

This photograph of Clayton's well-shaded Main Street at its intersection with Lombard Street appears in John T. Talton's 1909 *Illustrated Handbook of Clayton, North Carolina, and Vicinity*. At that time, Clayton was Johnston's largest town, with 1,441 residents counted in 1910. It had both cotton and tobacco markets, as well as markets for melons, lumber, fertilizers, and cotton-seed meal. A local telephone system connected Claytonites with folks in Raleigh, Smithfield, Wendell, Garner, Auburn, and other nearby towns. (Courtesy of Virginia Satterfield.)

This group of men and boys are assembled in front of Champion's store at the corner of Main and Church Streets in Clayton in the 1910s. (Courtesy of Virginia Satterfield.)

The Pythian Home was established at the outskirts of Clayton in 1911 by the Knights of Pythias as an orphanage for both boys and girls. This fraternal organization's Clayton branch began in 1903. Its first chancellor commander was J.M. Turley. The home closed in December 1969. (Courtesy of Durwood Barbour.)

John Bunyan Ferrell (left) operated this store in the 400 block of Clayton's Main Street from about 1910 to the late 1920s. This photograph was taken about 1920. Store clerk Dock Austin is pictured to Mr. Ferrell's right. (Courtesy of Rosalie Ferrell.)

This oil mill in Pine Level was established in 1902 and produced cottonseed oil. William Berry "Doc" Oliver later purchased controlling stock and added this to a growing list of successful agriculturally related enterprises that he owned. A fire destroyed most of the mill in 1962. (Courtesy of Durwood Barbour.)

Pine Lake's Godwin Brothers' Drug Store is listed in the North Carolina directories as early as 1906. This postcard scene, recorded in 1913, shows how early automobile owners took advantage of photograph opportunities. The printer made a mistake on this card by spelling the name of the store as "Goodwin"; however, Godwin is the lettering on the window. (Courtesy of Durwood Barbour.)

About 1917, these Pine Level men were grading a section of the Pine Level-Micro Road. The equipment was a kerosene-burning, steam-driven tractor pulling a rotary blade plow. The "Doc" Oliver Livery Stable is in the background. (Courtesy of North Carolina Division of Archives and History.)

B. Goodwin's Residence, Main Street, Pine Level, N. C.

This postcard, postmarked 1914, shows the home of Berry Godwin (misspelled on the card), still standing in Pine Level. Berry Godwin's son, Clyde, owned and operated a drugstore in Pine Level for many years. (Courtesy of Vernon Creech.)

Four
Atlantic Coastline Railroad Towns:
Kenly, Micro, Four Oaks, Benson

This postcard view of Main Street in Kenly was mailed in August 1913. Kenly, chartered in 1887, was named in honor of J.R. Kenly of the Wilmington and Weldon Railroad. The Hotel Glenn is partially shown on the left. Tin-covered, lean-to storefronts were a common sight well into the 1930s. (Courtesy of Durwood Barbour.)

This Queen Anne-style house on East Bailey Avenue in Kenly was built about the turn of the century by a Dr. Smith. Zebulon V. Snipes came to town as a bookkeeper and bought it in 1907. (Courtesy of Mrs. E.M. Rose.)

James Alvin Hodge, shown in the doorway, owned and operated this general merchandise store in Kenly about 1915. One of his best customers was the Dennis Simmons Lumber Company. They operated a tramway along a route that is now North Carolina 222, hauling virgin timber back to Kenly. (Courtesy of Ray Hodge.)

In 1906, William and John Edgerton built the Hotel Glenn, which was the pride of Kenly. It was named for Governor Glenn. The ground level contained several stores, the post office, a barber shop, and the hotel lobby. The hotel was upstairs. (Courtesy of Vernon Creech.)

Route 22 became U.S. 301 in 1935. This photograph of a motor court in Kenly was taken in the late 1930s. (Courtesy of Vernon Creech.)

In 1897, before the days of public high schools, brothers Bill and John Edgerton built Kenly's first school, the Kenly Academy, which was a boarding high school into the 1920s. Eventually sold to the County, the original wooden building became the teacher's residence for the new brick Kenly High School in 1914. (Courtesy of Durwood Barbour.)

The new brick Kenly High School was dedicated in May 1914. This was the same year Kenly got electric lights. (Courtesy of Durwood Barbour.)

This Micro School was built in 1905 for white students at a cost of $750. The school was located in District No. 9 of Beulah Township, and it had two rooms. It served Micro until the new school was completed in 1924. (Courtesy of Johnston County Room.)

The new brick school in Micro was completed in 1924. The teacher's residence on the left was erected in 1926. The first principal was C.H. Dula. The school was closed in 1987 and has since been dismantled. (Courtesy of Johnston County Room.)

Four Oaks received a municipal charter in 1889. It took its name from four trees growing from an oak stump on the Kinchen L. Barbour property. This postcard image was postmarked 1912 and shows the Barbour house on the left, built in 1885. Until 1909, the house was outside the

In 1910, the population of Four Oaks was 329. This postcard, mailed in 1912, shows a busy image for a small town. Policeman William Duncan "Bill Dunk" Stanley is second from right. Although not visible here, streetlights had been installed in 1907 and were left burning until 10 pm each night. (Courtesy of Durwood Barbour.)

town boundary. Barbour's wife died in 1910, and her sister, Ella Keene Williams, came to help him rear his children. Mr. Barbour built the house on the right for her. Both houses still stand, and the town now has a park on the property. (Courtesy of Dorcas Stanley Taylor.)

The D.H. Sanders Drug Company, shown here about 1910, was established in Four Oaks in 1904 by David H. Sanders (on the left) and Dr. John Haywood Stanley. In 1916 North Carolina required that prescriptions be compounded by licensed pharmacists, so in 1918 pharmacist Ralph Canaday bought an interest in the store. The name was then changed to Four Oaks Drug Company. (Courtesy of Lib Canaday.)

The Sandhill School, on South Main Street, was completed in 1907, a year before this photograph was taken. It was Four Oaks' second school and originally taught grades one through seven. Sometime prior to 1915, high school grades eight and nine were added. Sandhill closed in the spring of 1923, when the new brick school was completed. (Courtesy of Johnston County Room.)

The new brick school on the left opened on North Main Street in Four Oaks in 1923. The teacher's residence in the center was completed in 1927, and the class building on the right opened in 1934. In the mid-1930s, when consolidation of the small rural schools increased the enrollment to over 1,900, Four Oaks claimed the title of "Largest Rural Consolidated School in the World." N.C. Shuford moved from Sandhill School as principal the first year, and J.T. Hatcher served in that post from 1924 to 1954. On December 25, 1987, an arsonist set fire to the oldest building, and it burned to the ground. (Courtesy of North Carolina Division of Archives and History.)

This August 1941 picture of a Four Oaks school bus appeared in *National Geographic* as a part of an article about North Carolina. The bus route went northwest into Elevation Township. (Courtesy of Johnston County Room.)

Four Oaks (later called Forest Hills) School for black students was built in 1928, offering the elementary grades. Until 1961, Four Oaks students went to Johnston County Training School in Smithfield for high school diplomas. (Courtesy of North Carolina Division of Archives and History.)

This was Four Oaks' first firetruck, a 1930 Chevrolet. The backdrop is the high school building. Shown here are town leaders and members of the first fire department, which was organized in 1930. (Courtesy of Johnston County Room.)

About 1923, Albert Barden made a series of pictures for the Benson Kiwanis Club. They were made into a booklet used to promote Benson. In this photograph, the ACL train is making a stop. (Courtesy of North Carolina Division of Archives and History.)

Benson firemen tested their first pumper around 1907. It was horse drawn, and the pump was powered by gasoline. The Town purchased this equipment in 1907 and still owns it. The equipment is said to have been the first of its kind in North Carolina. The water was pumped from cisterns at four or five sites around town. (Courtesy of Harold Medlin.)

This photograph of the Rose and Woodall Company in Benson was made about 1923 by Albert Barden. It was a combination furniture and funeral business, which J.H. Rose established in 1905 as Rose and Company. The Rose family bought Will Woodall's interest in 1940, and they still operate the Rose and Graham Funeral Home on West Main Street. It was about 1922 that they began to offer embalming, eventually leading to the trend away from "do-it-yourself" burials. (Courtesy of North Carolina Division of Archives and History.)

The North State Hotel was located at the corner of Route 22 (U.S. 301) and Main Street in Benson. The train depot was a block away, making it convenient to both modes of travel. Alonzo Parrish built the hotel and also owned the Chevrolet dealership. The name was later changed to the Carolina Hotel. (Courtesy of North Carolina Division of Archives and History.)

The J.W. Whittenton Jewelry Store is shown here on Main Street in Benson in 1923. It was established in 1895 and is said to have been the first jewelry store in Johnston County. (Courtesy of North Carolina Division of Archives and History.)

In 1923, Main Street in Benson gave this view to the east from the railroad. Fires in 1894 and 1903 destroyed most of the early wooden structures, and they were replaced by brick buildings, such as the ones shown here. To the left, Jacob Woodall's family is carrying on the business he began in 1890. A dental office is upstairs over the Benson Drug Company. (Courtesy of North Carolina Division of Archives and History.)

The foundation for this Benson high school began in 1905. Students were enrolled from four counties. In 1917 the new brick school (now the municipal building) was built, and the old wooden structure became an apartment building on the next block. It was called the Dixie House and was dismantled in the early 1990s. (Courtesy of Harold Medlin.)

Benson area native Azel Manning (1878–1952), who called himself the King, the Prophet, the High Knocker of the Lord, became a well-known street preacher, traveling into twenty-eight states, usually by train and often without a ticket. Legend has assigned him hexing powers of mystical proportions. He made many headlines—once in *Life* magazine for crashing a United States Senate committee meeting. He made his living by selling produce and was especially well known for his cabbage plants. Here he is vending his wares behind a Model T Ford in the 1920s. (Courtesy of Johnston County Room.)

Five

Home Life

The Micajah and Mehettebell Jinnett Cox family of Bentonville Township posed for this photograph about 1896. In those days before stock laws, farm families maintained fences such as the one shown here around their homes and crops to keep out free-ranging livestock. (Courtesy of Johnston County Room.)

The home of John and Amy Harper was used as a hospital for Confederate and Union soldiers wounded in the last major battle of the Civil War at Bentonville. The house was owned by Samuel I. Thornton when this postcard was made, about 1905. This house is now part of the state's Bentonville Battleground historic site. (Courtesy of Durwood Barbour.)

This gathering of Harpers at Bentonville in 1893 is said to have been at the former slave quarters on the John and Amy Harper farm. (Courtesy of North Carolina Division of Archives and History.)

Members of the Sanders family of Cleveland Township posed with servants in front of their ancestral home, "Pleasant Grove," which is still standing on Cleveland Road. The original portion of the house was built for Col. John Sanders (1775–1830). The house was later enlarged by attaching another house which had been moved from a nearby site. (Courtesy of Johnston County Room.)

The Rains Lee family posed in front of their home in Ingrams Township's Blackman's Crossroads section about 1910. This two-room house, made of log and covered with clapboards, was typical of most Johnston County farm homes in the eighteenth and nineteenth centuries. At left is the porch-room, where travelers and other incidental guests were allowed to lodge. The Lees were among Johnston's many self-sufficient farmers who tended their land with family labor and produced almost everything they ate and wore. The daughters of this family were unique, however, in that they lived in this house until after World War II without plumbing, electricity, or any other modern convenience. (Courtesy of Jimmy Peacock.)

Some members of an unidentified tenant farm family are pictured here in front of the Moore-Yelvington house in Cleveland Township, around the turn of the century. (Courtesy of Ann Yelvington.)

This rare interior photograph shows the dining room of Dr. Richard J. Noble and Bettie Moore Noble's home in Selma c. 1920. The Nobles were among the first residents of Selma when the town was formed in 1867. Dr. Noble practiced medicine there for over a half-century, from the 1870s to the 1920s. (Courtesy of Richard J. Noble.)

Here are two additional views of the interior of the R.J. Noble home, Selma, *c.* 1920. (Courtesy of Richard J. Noble.)

Will Barbour was photographed feeding the cat at his father's, Kinchen L. Barbour, Four Oaks homestead around 1910. (Courtesy of Dorcas Stanley Taylor.)

Members of the Josephus Johnson family of Elevation Township are shown here making syrup, or homemade molasses, around the turn of the twentieth century. Edith Johnson described the process in a December 28, 1979 *Smithfield Herald* article. First, the cane was cut and brought to the shelter. Then, the fodder (seen covering the ground) was stripped, and the cane was fed into a mill (this one was steam powered) to crush it. The juice ran out into buckets and was cooked slowly until thick enough to sop, then placed in jars or barrels. A family member, second from left, is holding a device used to skim the foam from the top during the cooking process. (Courtesy of Edith Stephenson Johnson.)

People in town and country alike kept chickens in the yard to provide eggs and fresh poultry on the table. Sarah Woodall Hudson and her flock are shown at her home on South Third Street in Smithfield during feeding time around 1910. (Courtesy of Gordon Hudson.)

Sarah Hudson's son, Gardner, prepares the family garden plot for planting about 1910. (Courtesy of Gordon Hudson.)

Mrs. Hudson shows off the fruits of her labors. (Courtesy of Gordon Hudson.)

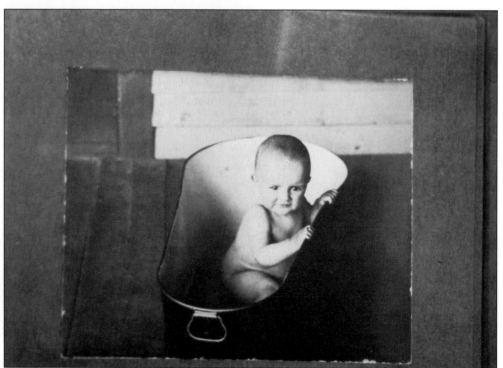

This unidentified baby, photographed in about 1910, is thought to be a neighbor of the Hudson family. (Courtesy of Gordon Hudson.)

This hog-killing is thought to have taken place on the Joseph and Helen Price farm in O'Neals Township sometime in the 1910s. (Courtesy of Thelma Bettis and Anne Cooke.)

Lottie Price (third from left) and three other ladies are pictured at the same hog-killing. Their job was to remove the entrails. (Courtesy of Thelma Bettis and Anne Cooke.)

About 1934, a group of Johnston County Home Demonstration Club members went to see the Washington, D.C. sights. Rachel Everett, the Home Demonstration agent who is standing at left, organized the trip. A few of the husbands went along also. (Courtesy of Johnston County Room.)

Six
Leisure

Brothers James B. (far left) and John H.B. Tomlinson (third from left) of Smithfield Township entertained visitors from Kingston, New York, in January 1897. These men, whom the Tomlinsons had befriended in their travels, made an annual stopover in Johnston County on their way to Florida. (Courtesy of John Hobart.)

About 1920, this Four Oaks baseball team was defeating Smithfield 10-2. The ball field is thought to have been located behind the Sandhill School, on South Main Street in Four Oaks. (Courtesy of Dorcas Stanley Taylor.)

The town of Princeton proudly fielded this baseball team *c.* 1915. (Courtesy of Maurice Toler.)

The Clayton High School Tennis Club of 1904–1905 posed on the steps of the dormitory at the corner of Fayetteville and Second Streets. (Courtesy of Virginia Satterfield.)

Members of Benson and Erwin baseball teams joined forces at the Benson field *c.* 1930 to play a formidable opponent. (Courtesy of Harold Medlin.)

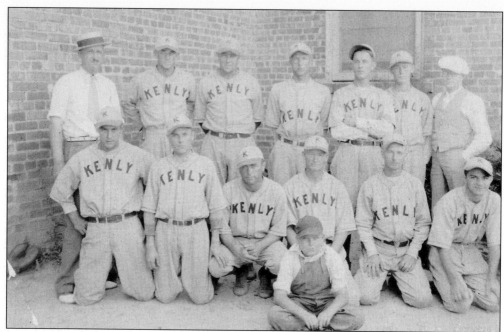

This Kenly semi-professional baseball team, pictured in the late 1920s, played in the Johnston County League. Al Evans (1916–1979), shown second from right in the back row, went on in 1939 to begin a twelve-year, 704-game professional career, mostly with the Washington Senators. (Courtesy of Johnston County Room.)

A Meadow School girls basketball team posed in 1935. (Courtesy of Harold Medlin.)

The 1938 Selma Cotton Mill baseball team posed here in their new uniforms on a ball field adjacent to the cotton mill warehouse. Known as the Cards, they played in the Johnston County League. Some of the players were employees of the mill. (Courtesy of Harry Hill.)

Smithfield High School's football team is pictured here during a 1934 practice session. (Courtesy of Edwin Matthews.)

Micro High School's 1935–1936 basketball team made their school proud by winning the county championship. (Courtesy of James W. Batten.)

Short Journey School's boys and girls basketball teams posed for this picture c. 1945. (Courtesy of the Johnston County Room.)

In the early twentieth century, Claytonites were able to enjoy frequent afternoon recitals by high school elocution classes such as this one pictured in 1904. Despite pleas by teacher Mrs. Robert F. Williams for aspiring business and professional men to sign up to improve their communication skills, this class was traditionally composed of all females. (Courtesy of Virginia Satterfield.)

H.P. Howell bought the Lyric Theatre in Smithfield in 1922, and changed the name to the Victory in 1924. Around 1923, he delighted townsfolk with lantern slides of local scenes and children. (Courtesy of Lucile Johnson Wallace.)

This sign at Smithfield's Market and Third Street intersection greeted visitors on their way to the 1920 County Fair. This event was held at the County Agricultural Society Fair Grounds, complete with racetrack and exhibit hall, located at the southeast corner of Holt and South Fifth Streets, on the outskirts of town. Exhibits included farm machinery, livestock, needlework, canned goods, students' creations, and musical instruments. One of the main attractions was a young lady diving 100 feet into a five-foot tank of water. (Courtesy of Johnston County Room.)

The Selma Tomato, Melon, and Better Baby Fair was held each year between 1912 and 1917. It was promoted by John A. Mitchener. Thirty to fifty babies under the age of twelve months competed for cash prizes: (Courtesy of Sarah Manning Pope.)

A handsome float with a bevy of pretty southern belles waits for the parade to begin at the 1915 Selma Tomato, Melon, and Better Baby Fair. (Courtesy of Eunice Temple Kirkpatrick.)

The Star Minstrels were a group of Smithfield actors who performed humorous black-face skits in the 1890s. The March 17, 1892 *Smithfield Herald* stated that their performance in that year was held in the courthouse for the benefit of local churches. (Courtesy of Susie Johnson.)

Jubilant marchers made their way down Benson's Main Street for an Armistice Day parade around 1919. (Courtesy of Harold Medlin.)

Virtually every inch of this automobile was decorated for the Benson Armistice Day parade. (Courtesy of Harold Medlin.)

This photograph shows only a small portion of the twenty thousand people in attendance at Benson's Annual Singing Convention in June 1938. On stage at the East Main Street singing grove are the East Burlington Girls Quartet. This gospel music festival began in 1921, largely through the efforts of Simon Honeycutt, and continues annually each June. (Courtesy of *News and Observer* and North Carolina Division of Archives and History.)

This unidentified choir competed for a trophy at the 1938 Benson Singing Convention. (Courtesy of *News and Observer* and North Carolina Division of Archives and History.)

The 1932 Four Oaks Toy Band posed on the steps of the school with a variety of percussion instruments. (Courtesy of Dorcas Stanley Taylor.)

The Princeton Town Band provided music for concerts and special events throughout the county. They posed for this picture on the steps of a Clayton school in 1927. (Courtesy of Maurice Toler.)

Short Journey School's Glee Club is shown here in this *c.* 1945 photograph. (Courtesy of Johnston County Room.)

Bill Joe Austin (1911–1991) loved music, and he spent a lifetime honing his skill with a saxophone. Austin and his orchestra played Sunday afternoons and Wednesday nights at Holt's Lake for several summers beginning in 1936. Here on the Holt's Lake pavilion, their fans are not dancing, since management would not allow it on Sundays. (Courtesy of Lucile McLemore Austin.)

Smithfield High School band leader George Groves, his band, and drum and bugle corps are pictured here as they marched on the school grounds in about 1933. (Courtesy of Hubert Woodall Jr.)

On a Sunday afternoon about 1919, Claude Stephenson's Uncle Israel Stephenson and his children Bessie and Herman came to visit at his home in Pleasant Grove Township. In this photograph, they, along with Claude's daughters Claudia and Edith, are examining a wooden-slatted fish trap made by Claude's brother, Richard Stephenson, on a Middle Creek dam. (Courtesy of Claudia Stephenson Brown.)

Fishing at ponds such as this one at Holt's Mill near Princeton has been a favorite pastime from earliest settlement. This pre-1920s photograph shows the Atlantic Coastline Railroad's Goldsboro-to-Smithfield line, which once crossed over Holt's Pond. Built by the short-lived North Carolina Midland Railroad, most locals called it "Captain Jack's Railroad," in honor of conductor Jack Collier. (Courtesy of Mrs. Leo Woodard.)

J.H.B. Tomlinson (left) and David Smith took time to reward their hunting dogs at the Walter Myatt farm in Cleveland Township around 1897. (Courtesy of John Hobart.)

Family reunions have been popular summer pastimes for many generations of Johnstonians, particularly since the Industrial Revolution of the late nineteenth century began to put greater distances between family members. This gathering of the William Joseph Woodard family of Boon Hill Township took place sometime in the 1920s. (Courtesy of Mrs. Leo Woodard.)

Mr. and Mrs. George Thornton; their son, Everett; and niece, Julia Rose, enjoy a leisurely Sunday afternoon buggy excursion on the outskirts of South Smithfield about 1905. (Courtesy of Julia Rose.)

The banks of rivers and creeks afforded opportunities to fish and ponder. Gardner Hudson is enjoying the serenity of the Neuse at Smithfield in this *c.* 1910 photograph. (Courtesy of Gordon Hudson.)

The creativity and ingenuity of an unidentified toy maker are captured in this photograph of a miniature locomotive of the 1910s. The child is also unidentified, but is thought to have been photographed in the vicinity of South Third and Woodall Streets in Smithfield. (Courtesy of Gordon Hudson.)

These Smithfield boys brought at least one of the comforts of home (their beds) to this camping experience in the 1910s. (Courtesy of Gordon Hudson.)

A serviceman from Goldsboro met this group of Clayton girls and their chaperone with a bus to take them to a dance at Seymour Johnson about 1942. They always met at this Sinclair service station at the corner of Main and Church Streets on Friday nights. The chaperone was Carmine Satterfield (extreme left). (Courtesy of Virginia Satterfield.)

Seven
Making a Living

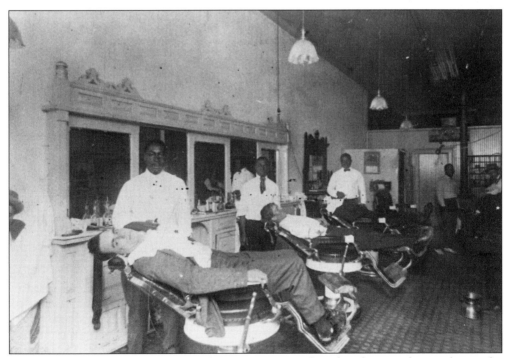

Haywood Smith had a barber shop in the Tuscarora Inn when this photograph was taken in the early 1920s. The photograph was made into a lantern slide and shown at the local movie theater. (Courtesy of Lucile Johnson Wallace.)

Ner Hatcher (left) and his helper worked the hot iron into a horseshoe or other utilitarian shape at his blacksmith shop in Selma in 1905. (Courtesy of James W. Batten.)

P.B. Johnson sold farm supplies, wagons, and other farming implements in Benson. Here is an inside view of the nerve center of his operation *c.* 1923. (Courtesy of North Carolina Division of Archives and History.)

Former slave Ellen Turner Mitchiner (*c.* 1844–1932) was a well-known midwife in the Wilson's Mills vicinity in the late nineteenth and early twentieth centuries. According to grand-niece Elsie Collins, if a mother was too ill to care for the baby or if the mother died, Mrs. Mitchiner brought the baby home and searched for a family who would provide foster care. She worked with Dr. Charles Furlonge after he came to Johnston County in 1916, and was certified by the State Board of Health after the state began requiring certification for midwives in 1919. (Courtesy of Elsie Collins.)

In 1931, the staff of the Johnston County Hospital assembled at the entrance for this photograph. (Courtesy of Johnston County Room.)

This is a photograph of a load of fodder at Joe Woodard's place in Boon Hill Township in the early 1900s. Fodder was produced by pulling green corn leaves, tying them into bundles, and hanging them on corn stalks to dry. West Woodard is standing, and Joe Woodard is seated. (Courtesy of Mrs. Leo Woodard.)

Teams of mules and oxen pulled pine logs to the Brown Siding on Jack's Railroad in the early 1900s. The siding was near Braswell's Store and Princeton. Cutting of pine trees often followed the turpentine harvests. (Courtesy of Mrs. Leo Woodard.)

Members of Boon Hill Township's Lynch, Tyner, and Worley families were part of this logging crew on the Neuse Islands in the early twentieth century. Besides providing timber, this rugged, swampy terrain (also called the Mashes) was also a place where moonshiners and fugitives from the law were known to hide out. (Courtesy of Westa Talton Morris.)

In April 1914, everybody paused for the photographer at Will Tomlinson's cotton gin in Cleveland Township. The photograph shows Tomlinson on the buggy and at least three species of animals—horses, mules, and oxen—being used to transport workers and cotton. (Courtesy of Charles Tomlinson.)

In December 1915, four mules were photographed hauling twenty bales of cotton to market on Smithfield's Market Street. The cotton came from Will Tomlinson's gin, located 6 miles away in Cleveland Township. After being weighed, the load turned out to be worth $1,060 in cash. (Courtesy of Charles Tomlinson.)

Billy Langdon of Four Oaks photographed this tobacco-barning scene in 1906 on David Massengill's farm near Four Oaks. Tobacco farmers were in the minority at that time, since cotton was still king in Johnston County. (Courtesy of Janet Barbour.)

Somewhere in Johnston County, this steam shovel bucket was cutting its way through a grade on the Atlantic Coastline Railroad in preparation for a second track, *c.* 1920. (Courtesy of Harold Medlin.)

Along a Johnston County Road *c.* 1920, a crew is "pulling the ditches" to reshape a soil road. The kerosene-burning, steam-propelled tractor is towing a bladed grader. The man on the grader is training his child at a very early age. (Courtesy of Harold Medlin.)

Albert Barden took this photograph in the early 1940s of tobacco planting or "setting" in Johnston County. In a few short years, these mules would be replaced by small farm tractors. A few years prior to this, most tobacco was planted by hand using wooden pegs. (Courtesy of North Carolina Division of Archives and History.)

The wheat harvest on the Phillip Lee farm in Ingrams Township was truly a family endeavor when this photograph was taken in 1908. (Courtesy of Johnston County Room.)

Here, Lester Massengill of Four Oaks, RFD No. 2, is plowing his corn *c.* 1908. In a corn-growing contest sponsored by the State Agriculture Department, Lester placed first, ahead of sixteen other boys in the county. His prize was $35 worth of fertilizer. (Courtesy of Johnston County Room.)

On the day in September 1922 that the new Johnston County courthouse was dedicated, this group of men assembled to be recognized and to participate. The group includes members of the Johnston County Bar, county commissioners, court officials, and others. Colonel E.S. Abell presented the courthouse to the court, and it was accepted by Judge Frank A. Daniels. (Courtesy of Reuben Johnson.)

Clayton Oil Mill, built by A.J. Barbour in 1903, is shown here around 1909. A 1908 state labor report shows that this steam-powered plant employed twenty-eight men, who generally worked twelve-hour days for wages of 90¢ up to $1.60 a day. Their product was cottonseed oil. They compacted the husks and sold them to farmers as a supplementary livestock feed. (Courtesy of Johnston County Room.)

The Smithfield Cotton Mills was chartered, capital raised through stock sales, and the first mill and tenement houses were built in 1900. The contractor was D.J. Rose of Rocky Mount. Operation of the mill began in 1901. This was Johnston County's first cotton mill, and it was located on the east side of the railroad, just off Brogden Road. On March 21, 1925, the mill was destroyed by fire. (Courtesy of Johnston County Room.)

This interior view of the Ivanhoe Cotton Mill No. 2 was photographed in the 1920s. The corner of Brightleaf Boulevard (Hwy 301) and North Street is now the location of Burlington Mills in Smithfield. (Courtesy of James A. Wellons Jr.)

A tobacco auction is shown in progress in the autumn of 1935 at the Wallace warehouse on Smithfield's Third Street (behind the present-day Belk store and public library). Shown are warehouse owners Dixon Wallace (far left), brother Holton Wallace (third from left), and auctioneer Gunter Cooke (second from left). (Courtesy of Christine Rose Pines.)

Here, a Model T Ford truck of 1917–1923 vintage delivers hay to the H.D. Ellington Horse Stables. The stables were located on South Fourth Street in Smithfield, next to a laundry at Spring Branch. (Courtesy of Johnston County Room.)

During World War I, with the men away, Edith Powell of Bentonville Township took on extra responsibilities. Here this farmeress cultivates the corn crop with some well-fed mules. Edith later became Mrs. H.V. Rose. (Courtesy of Willie M. Gaskin.)

Ladies working in this Clayton sewing room were pictured around 1904. Kerosene lamps were available to shed light on the work. (Courtesy of Hocutt-Ellington Memorial Library.)

A WPA project is captured in progress about 1940. It is believed to be the construction of the U.S. 301 Truck Lane through Smithfield. The foreman and helpers appear to be installing grade level stakes for roadway construction. The photograph was taken by Hooks Studio. (Courtesy of Mary Frances Bingham.)

S.C. Turnage and Ralph Talton are shown at their grocery store on Third Street in Smithfield in the early 1920s. This photograph was made into a lantern slide and shown at the theatre in 1923. (Courtesy of Lucile Johnson Wallace.)

This is said to have been taken inside the Ashley Smith store at the northeast corner of Market and Third Streets. The building, shown on a Sanborn insurance map as early as 1885, housed a dry goods store in the 1880s and 1890s and also a general merchandise establishment in the 1890s and early 1900s. By about 1915, when this photograph was taken, it was the Smith grocery store. The woman behind the counter is thought to be Mrs. Lina Smith. The building was razed in 1935. (Courtesy of Travis Frierson.)

The interior of the Farmers' Bank and Trust Company in Smithfield left this image on a lantern slide in 1923. Located next to the courthouse, the building was later purchased by First Citizens Bank. Racially segregated examining rooms in the rear were used for private viewing of safe deposit box contents. (Courtesy of Lucile Johnson Wallace.)

The J.D. Spiers Store, built in 1906, carried a full line of clothing at Market and Third Streets. This picture, dating from about 1920, shows Mr. Spiers at back center. The building later became Gregory's 10 Cent Store. (Courtesy of Lucile Johnson Wallace.)

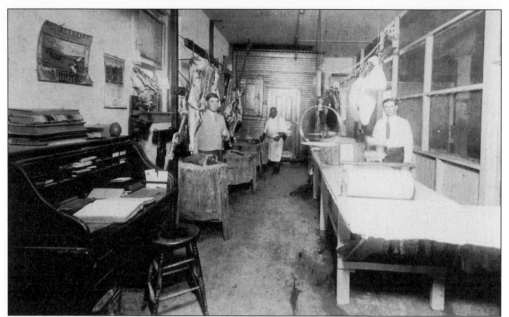

This photograph dating from the early 1920s is of M.B. Strickland's meat market, on the first floor of the town hall and opera house on Smithfield's Third Street. Strickland is at left front, and butcher Less Drew is in back. Well-known photographer Reuben Johnson recalled working there in those days before refrigeration. His job entailed delivering meat practically all night on Saturdays so Smithfield folks could have it fresh for their Sunday dinners. (Courtesy of James A. Wellons Jr.)

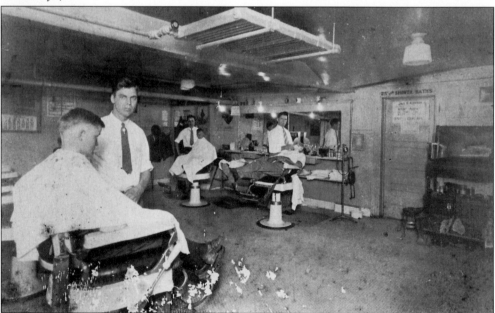

About 1935, this photograph recorded an important moment in the everyday life of boys and men—a shave and a haircut. The shop was located in the basement of the Hood Building, at the corner of Market and Third Streets. Ronnie Narron is the barber in the foreground. (Courtesy of Johnston County Room.)

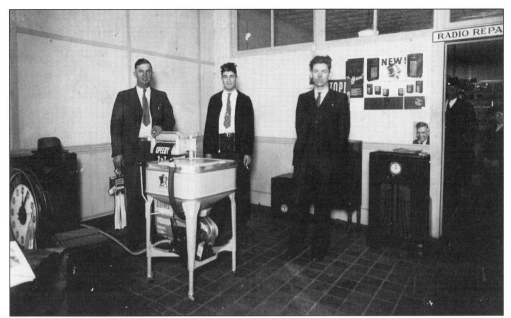

Denton F. Lee Sr., Smithfield's first radio and appliance dealer, opened Radio Sales and Service in 1934. By 1939, he had moved to his new building, shown here at 136 South Third Street, where the old opera house once stood. When he expanded his sales to television and other appliances in the late 1940s, the name was changed to Denton F. Lee Appliances. Lee (right) is standing with two salesmen, who are demonstrating the latest model Maytag washing machine. (Courtesy of Margaret McLemore Lee.)

Jesse Stanley began his automobile business in Four Oaks in the 1920s. Later he moved to a more lucrative site in Smithfield. Here is his showroom in Smithfield with the new 1934 models. The center car is a Chrysler Airflow, and the one on the right is a Dodge. The Airflow was of such radical design that it did not sell well and was made for only two years. (Courtesy of Dorcas Stanley Taylor.)

In 1938, Medlin Printing Company was located at the corner of Fourth and Market Streets in Smithfield. Ira W. Medlin (seated at typesetter) started this family business in 1924, and his son, Thomas E. (standing in foreground), succeeded him. The company now includes a third generation of Medlins. (Courtesy of Calvin Edgerton.)

Fanny Allen Morgan was a former slave living in Smithfield and working for the A.M. Sanders family on Hancock Street in the early 1930s when captured in this photograph. Known for her mouth-watering fried chicken, she is on her way home with a basket of leftovers. (Courtesy of Marsha Hood Brewer.)

Eight
Making a Difference

Governor Benjamin Williams (1751–1814), North Carolina's only chief executive from Johnston County so far, distinguished himself as both a politician and Revolutionary War patriot. He was governor for two terms, 1799–1802 and 1807–1808. He served several terms in both houses of the state legislature, and one term in the U.S. Congress (1793–1795). Williams was one of the first trustees of the University of North Carolina in 1789, and he played a major role in selecting Chapel Hill as the site in 1792. (Courtesy of Johnston County Room.)

Dr. Calvin Jones (1775–1846), a native of Massachusetts, became a noted pioneer in the use of Edward Jenner's smallpox vaccine and in eye surgery while he was practicing medicine in Smithfield between 1795 and 1803. While representing Johnston County in the State House of Commons in 1802, he introduced the first bill to establish free schools in North Carolina. The bill was defeated, but Jones's dream was finally realized almost four decades later, when the General Assembly of 1839 passed legislation allowing counties to provide public schools. (Courtesy of North Carolina Division of Archives and History.)

Dr. James Thomas Leach Sr. (1805–1883) was a noted physician, planter, politician, and lifelong resident of Johnston County's Cleveland Township. In 1863, he was elected to the Confederate Congress in Richmond, where he lobbied without success for an early end to the Civil War. After the war, he served as county commissioner (chairman, 1872–1873) and led local prohibition forces, who were voted down in an 1881 referendum. (Courtesy of Evelyn McCullers Sherratt.)

Clayton's Andrew Jackson "Jack" Ellis (1847–1944), second from left, posed with son, Wade, and local dignitaries F.H. Brooks and H.V. Rose around 1943 while being honored as Johnston County's last surviving Confederate veteran. He enlisted with the Junior Reserves at age seventeen and was home on sick furlough when he heard cannons firing at the Battle of Bentonville. A skirmish followed soon thereafter in a grove near his family's farmstead in which one Union soldier was killed and another wounded. His mother helped in caring for these enemy soldiers, only to have another group of men in blue steal her chickens and slice ham from live pigs, leaving the pigs' carcasses in the field. (Courtesy of Johnston County Room.)

This gathering of former Confederate soldiers around the turn of the century is most likely a reunion of North Carolina's 31st Regiment, Company D, an infantry unit primarily composed of Johnston and Wake County men. This company participated in battles at Roanoke Island, White Hall, Battery Wagner, Batchelder's Creek, Plymouth, Drewry's Bluff, Cold Harbor, Petersburg, Globe Tavern, Fort Harrison, 2nd Fort Fisher, and Bentonville. (Courtesy of Grace Laughter Barbour.)

Rev. Jesse Wheeler (1837–1914), Confederate veteran and cousin of President Andrew Johnson, was a circuit-riding missionary to the Choctaw and Chickasaw tribes in Atoka, Oklahoma, from the 1880s to the early 1900s. Wheeler was a charter member of Cleveland Township's Shiloh Baptist Church in 1860 and was licensed to preach there. Seated second from left, he is pictured with his family in Oklahoma around the turn of the century. (Courtesy of Marianne Wheeler.)

John C. Scarborough (1841–1917), Confederate veteran and educator who lived most of his adult life in Selma, served as North Carolina's superintendent of public instruction from 1877 to 1885 and as Johnston County's superintendent of schools from 1885 to 1887. He was a noted champion of the Blair Bill for federally-funded public schools, which was debated in Congress throughout the entire decade of the 1880s before finally being rejected. (Courtesy of North Carolina Division of Archives and History.)

Lunsford Richardson (1854–1919), inventor of Vicks VapoRub, began his career as a teacher, but left the education field in the early 1880s to open a drugstore in Selma. It was there that he reportedly concocted his famous salve. Relocating to Greensboro in 1890, he developed a line of products called Vicks, named in honor of his brother-in-law, Dr. Joshua Vick of Selma. Dropping all of this product line except VapoRub, the Richardsons eventually made Vicks a household word across America. (Courtesy of Johnston County Room.)

Governor William Carey Renfrow (1845–1922), chief executive of the Oklahoma Territory from 1893 to 1897, was born in Smithfield and served in the Confederate army. In 1865, he and his friend, Ransom Gulley of Clayton, sought fortunes in Arkansas. When the Oklahoma territory was opened in 1889, he moved there and began amassing a fortune in the livery business and in banking. Though not well known in the new territory, he reportedly won the gubernatorial appointment from President Grover Cleveland because of his financial success and clean reputation. (Courtesy of Oklahoma Historical Society, Archives and Manuscripts Division.)

Willis W. "Bud" Cole (1868–1924), Bentonville Township native and Smithfield attorney, was presiding over the county's Democratic Party Convention in 1900 when captured in this photograph. That year was a turning point for his party in Johnston County, marking the beginning of almost a century of Democratic political dominance. (Courtesy of Mrs. Hugh McGowan.)

Edward William Pou Jr. (1863–1934), lawyer, Democratic Party leader, and U.S Congressman, was born in Alabama but lived most of his life in his mother's native Johnston County. He served as solicitor (prosecuting attorney) for North Carolina's 4th Judicial District from 1890 to 1900. In 1901 he began a thirty-three-year career in the U.S. House of Representatives, serving as House rules chairman under Presidents Woodrow Wilson and Franklin D. Roosevelt. (Courtesy of Johnston County Room.)

Benjamin D. Creech was a farmer who was also serving as Benson's chief of police when he and his wife, Bettie, posed for this photograph around 1912. His beat contained eight hundred residents and included five churches, one school, one bank, two drugstores, thirty-two general merchandisers, four doctors, one dentist, three hotels, three livery stables, and several lumber mills. (Courtesy of Harold Medlin.)

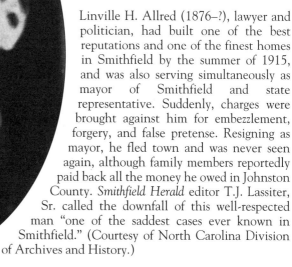

Linville H. Allred (1876–?), lawyer and politician, had built one of the best reputations and one of the finest homes in Smithfield by the summer of 1915, and was also serving simultaneously as mayor of Smithfield and state representative. Suddenly, charges were brought against him for embezzlement, forgery, and false pretense. Resigning as mayor, he fled town and was never seen again, although family members reportedly paid back all the money he owed in Johnston County. *Smithfield Herald* editor T.J. Lassiter, Sr. called the downfall of this well-respected man "one of the saddest cases ever known in Smithfield." (Courtesy of North Carolina Division of Archives and History.)

By the summer of 1917, men such as these Johnston County World War I inductees in Selma were bidding farewell to loved ones and boarding trains, each man bound for an uncertain future on the other side of the Atlantic. Johnston County sent almost one thousand of its sons and daughters to the war, and lost over fifty. Many came back from the war, but found jobs in other locales. (Courtesy of Art Andrews.)

Members of the Smithfield Chapter of the American Red Cross are pictured here at what is thought to have been the opening of the 1918 tobacco market. They raised funds by soliciting donations of tobacco from both local farmers and buyers in Smithfield warehouses. The money, supplemented by dues of $1 a year, aided the endeavors of the larger parent organization and purchased materials local members used in making hospital garments, bandages, dressings, and care packages for soldiers in France. (Courtesy of Johnston County Room.)

"Good Roads" Governor Cameron Morrison (in front, seventh from left, with jacket open), his council of state, and scores of lesser dignitaries attended a 1923 fish fry and barbecue to promote the Democratic Party and officially open Holt's Lake in its fourth season of fishing, swimming, boating, and picnicking. After consuming a feast of barbecued pig and some four hundred fried perch, the group listened to numerous lengthy political speeches, the first one offered by the governor, with lighted cigar in hand. (Courtesy of the Johnston County Room.)

Luma McLamb Merritt (1902–1995), a Benson area native, won the distinction of being Johnston County's first woman to hold elected office. She won the bid for register of deeds in 1928 on the Republican ticket, serving one four-year term. She later married and moved to Richmond, Virginia, where she spent most of her adult life. (Courtesy of Vila McLamb.)

Liquor still raids have been common occurrences in Johnston County ever since 1908, when a prohibition referendum passed. Johnston gained the title, "Banner Whiskey County," for its opposition to prohibition in 1908. Here, local law enforcement and government officials in the 1930s display with pride their latest spoils in the war on liquor. (Courtesy of Harold Medlin.)

William Edward Dodd (1869–1940), a Clayton-area native, was a noted educator, historian, and diplomat. He taught history at Randolph-Macon College in Ashland, Virginia, from 1900 to 1908, and at the University of Chicago from 1908 to 1932. In 1933, President Franklin D. Roosevelt appointed him ambassador to Germany. His Jeffersonian ideals clashed with both embassy staff and Nazi officials, leading to his being recalled in 1937. A prolific writer of history, he left behind numerous works on the American South. (Courtesy of Johnston County Room.)

Albert Coates (1896–1989), a Pleasant Grove Township native, founded the widely acclaimed Institute of Government at the University of North Carolina at Chapel Hill in 1931. A graduate of UNC and Harvard Law School, he taught in the UNC Law School from 1923 to 1969. (Courtesy of Johnston County Room.)

Hunter Johnson (born in 1906), an Elevation Township native and renowned composer, won the prestigious Prix de Rome in 1933, and then spent the next two years in Europe, studying composition in Rome. Here he is shown at the grave of English poet John Keats in 1935, shortly before Johnson's return to the United States. He won two Guggenheim Fellowships (1941, 1954) and taught composition at various American universities before retiring in 1971. His best known works are Piano Sonata (1934) and music he wrote for the Martha Graham ballets, Letter to the World (1940) and Deaths and Entrances (1943). (Courtesy of Johnston County Room.)

125

John Wesley Wood (born in 1917) of Banner Township enlisted in the U.S. Army in 1942 and sold his new 1942 Ford to buy $2,000 worth of war bonds. (Courtesy of John W. Wood.)

Talmadge Sanders (1926–?), called Dukie by friends and family, attended the Four Oaks School for black students before entering the Navy during World War II. His young life was one of those sacrificed overseas for the cause of democracy. (Courtesy of Annie Evans Walker.)

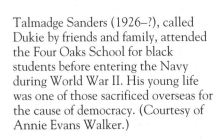

Richard Raynor (1919–?) was a member of the first student body at the Four Oaks School for blacks in 1928. He later paid the supreme sacrifice on the battlefields of North Africa during World War II. (Courtesy of Annie Evans Walker.)

Thurman White Peedin (1913–1981) of Boon Hill Township made the cover of *Life* magazine in the summer of 1944, after helping a wounded comrade near Naples, Italy. According to his son, Wayne, Peedin never knew the other soldier's name, since they were in different units. The two were returning from patrol when Peedin noticed the man was limping and using his rifle as a crutch, so Peedin naturally offered to help him get back to camp. It was not until he returned home that he learned about the magazine. (From *Life*, July 3, 1944.)

127

Henry E. Royall (born in 1904) of Boon Hill Township, is pictured here when he became Johnston County's first graduate of the United States Military Academy at West Point, New York, in 1930. As a senior at Smithfield High School in 1925, his principal helped him get the necessary recommendation from Congressman Pou. Attaining the rank of colonel in the U.S. Army, he retired in 1947 and now makes his home in Chapel Hill. (Courtesy of Henry E. Royall.)

Elreta Melton Alexander Ralston (born in 1919) was born in Smithfield while her father was pastor of First Missionary Baptist Church. After leaving the county, she became the first African-American woman to graduate from Columbia University School of Law in 1945. She later won the distinctions of being the first black woman lawyer and the first black woman judge in North Carolina. She is retired and lives in Greensboro. (Courtesy of Johnston County Room.)